Animal Poems of the Iguazú

Animalario del Iguazú

Poems / Poemas
Francisco X. Alarcón

Illustrations / Ilustraciones
Maya Christina Gonzalez

Children's Book Press
an imprint of Lee & Low Books Inc.
New York

Introducción

Estos poemas bilingües celebran una de las maravillas naturales del mundo —las Cataratas del Iguazú— localizadas en el noreste de Argentina, en la frontera con Brasil y Paraguay. Escribí la mayoría de estos poemas en un cuadernito verde durante mis visitas allí.

Las Cataratas del Iguazú han encantado a los indígenas de la región —los guaraníes— y a muchísimos otros visitantes a través de los siglos. El Parque Nacional Iguazú se estableció en 1934 para proteger las Cataratas del Iguazú y la selva subtropical a su alrededor. Este parque alberga miles de especies de árboles, plantas, aves, mamíferos, reptiles, anfibios e insectos. Es también uno de los ambientes naturales de mayor diversidad biológica del mundo.

Pero muchas de estas especies, tanto de animales como de plantas, están en peligro, algunas de ellas hasta amenazadas con extinción. La selva misma está en peligro. Organizaciones ecologistas de Argentina y del resto del mundo han propuesto la creación de un gran "corredor verde" trinacional que protegería casi 1,400,000 hectáreas de selva continua, uniendo el Parque Nacional Iguazú con otras áreas protegidas en el noreste de Argentina, y conectándolas con Puerto Bertoni en Paraguay y el Parque Nacional do Iguaçú de Brasil.

Sólo así podremos conservar *Ybirá Retá* ("Tierra de los Árboles" en la lengua guaraní) para las futuras generaciones. Espero que estos poemas nos motiven a todos a tomar acción para proteger las plantas y los animales silvestres del área del Iguazú y del mundo entero.

—*Francisco X. Alarcón*

Introduction

These bilingual poems celebrate one of the wonders of the natural world: the Iguazú Waterfalls, located in northeastern Argentina, along the border of Brazil and Paraguay. I wrote most of these poems in a small green notebook during my visits there.

The Iguazú Waterfalls have enchanted the indigenous people of the region—the Guaraní—and many other visitors for centuries. The Iguazú National Park was established in 1934 to protect the Iguazú Waterfalls and the surrounding subtropical rainforest. In this park there are literally thousands of species of trees, plants, birds, mammals, reptiles, amphibians, and insects. This park holds some of the greatest biological diversity in the world.

But many of these species—both animals and plants—are in serious danger, and some are even threatened with extinction. The rainforests themselves are in danger. Environmental organizations in Argentina and worldwide have proposed the creation of a great tri-national "green corridor" that would protect almost 1,400,000 hectares of continuous rainforest, joining the Iguazú National Park with other protected areas in northeastern Argentina, as well as Puerto Bertoni in Paraguay and the Iguaçú National Park in Brazil.

Only in this way will we be able to preserve *Ybirá Retá* ("Land of the Trees" in the Guaraní language) for future generations. I hope these poems will motivate all of us to take action to protect the wild animals and plants of the Iguazú area and of the entire world.

—*Francisco X. Alarcón*

Cataratas del Iguazú

Iguazú significa
"aguas grandes"
en guaraní

estas cataratas
son la gran risa
verdiazul

de la Madre Tierra
que se desgaja
en carcajadas —

en este paraíso
de plantas y animales
llamado Iguazú

cada día
ofrece más colores
que el arco iris

Iguazú Waterfalls

Iguazú means
"big waters"
in Guaraní

these waterfalls
are the big blue
and green laughter

of Mother Earth
cascading down
in loud peals—

in this paradise
of plants and animals
called Iguazú

every day
offers more colors
than the rainbow

Tucán
de pico tengo
dos rebanadas
de papaya

Toucan
for a beak
I have two
papaya slices

6

Yacaré
(Caiman)

on the rocks
of the Iguazú river
I'll always lie

under the sun
a smiling happy
caiman

Yacaré
(Caimán)

sobre rocas
del río Iguazú
me echaré

siempre al sol
sonriendo feliz
como yacaré

en el cielo   me pongo   a danzar

Jote

la jota circular   de buitres   y zopilotes

up in the sky   I dance   la jota

Jote

the sweeping circles   of vultures   and buzzards

Loro
tengo
un pecho
multicolor

y un pico
cotorro
muy hablador

Parrot
I have
a multicolored
breast

and a very
loquacious
little beak

Picaflor

vuelo
vuelo
vuelo

pico
pico
pico

muchas flores
pues eso soy
un picaflor

Hummingbird

I flit
flit
flit

I pick
pick
pick

many flowers
I'm a flower-picking
hummingbird

Golondrina parda*

las largas alas
de mi cuerpo pardo
aerodinámico

me impiden posarme
en los árboles
o sobre la tierra

por eso hago nido
en los muros rocosos
de altos desfiladeros

por detrás del velo
de las cascadas velo
por este parque nacional

Great Dusky Swift**

the long wings
of my aerodynamic
dusky body

don't allow me
to perch in trees
or on the ground

that's why I nest
on the rocky walls
of high cliffs

from behind the veil
of the falls I watch
over this national park

* La golondrina parda es parte del emblema oficial del Parque Nacional Iguazú.
** The great dusky swift is part of the official emblem of the Iguazú National Park.

Mito guaraní

todas las nubes
del cielo nacen
de la matriz

de la catarata
más grande
del río Iguazú

desde lejos
columnas de vapor
ascienden al cielo

Guaraní Myth

the sky's clouds
are all born
from the womb

of the largest
Iguazú river
waterfall

from afar
columns of mist
rise to the sky

De azul

una creencia común
de la gente
guaraní

es que Dios pintó
el cielo de color azul
lleno de inspiración

con el extracto
de la semillita
del *ñangapirí*

Blue Job

a common belief
of the Guaraní
people

is that God
painted the sky
an inspiring blue

with the extract
from the tiny
ñangapirí seed

Coatí

un coatí soy
muy orgulloso
de mi gran cola

muy curioso
muy hambriento
con mi gran nariz

voy olfateando
la comida que sé
que todos cargan

Coatí

I'm a coatí
very proud
of my great tail

so curious
so hungry
with my big nose

sniffing out
the food I know
you all carry

Lagartija

en una escapada
peligrosa hasta
mi cola verde perdí

pero como lagartija
todavía puede
volver a crecer

Lizard

in a dangerous
escape I lost
my green tail

but as a lizard
I can still
grow it back

Las mariposas
somos las flores
multicolores
del aire

Butterflies
we are
the multicolored
flowers of the air

Martín Pescador*

mi nombre
completo es
Martín Pescador

porque pescar
es lo que más
me gusta a mí

no necesito
caña ni red
pues tengo ojos

y un gran pico
listos para ricos
peces atrapar

Martín Pescador**

my full Spanish name
is Martín Pescador
or "Martin Fisher"

because fishing
is what I enjoy
the most

I don't need
a rod or a net
for I have eyes

and a big beak
ready to catch
some tasty fish

* Martín pescador es el pájaro hábil en la pesca conocido en inglés como *kingfisher*.
** *Martín pescador* is the skillful fishing bird known as "kingfisher" in English.

Jaguareté
(Jaguar)

dicen que ahora
estoy casi extinto
por este parque

pero la gente
que dice esto
no sabe

que al oler
las orquídeas
en los árboles

están percibiendo
la fragancia
de mis fauces

que al oír
el retumbo
de los saltos

están escuchando
el gran rugido
de mis ancestros

que al observar
las constelaciones
del firmamento

están mirando
las motas de estrellas
marcadas en mi piel

que yo soy
y siempre seré
el indomable

espíritu
silvestre vivo
de esta jungla

Jaguareté
(Jaguar)

some say
I'm now almost
extinct in this park

but the people
who say this
don't know

that by smelling
the orchids
in the trees

they're sensing
the fragrance
of my chops

that by hearing
the rumbling
of the waterfalls

they're listening
to my ancestors'
great roar

that by observing
the constellations
of the night sky

they're gazing
at the star spots
on my fur

that I am and
always will be
the wild

untamed
living spirit
of this jungle

¡Qué plaga!

qué plaga más plaga
estos grandes mosquitos
con ruidosos motores

del lado brasileño
del Parque Nacional
Iguazú

¡cómo nos molestan
a las aves en nido
estos helicópteros

con humanos que
ni siquiera pueden
por sí solos volar!

What a Pest!

what huge pests
these big mosquitos
with noisy motors

high on the Brazilian
side of the Iguazú
National Park

we nesting birds
get really annoyed
by these helicopters

carrying humans
who can't fly
by themselves!

Hormigas gigantes

desde nuestros miradores
las hormigas podemos
divisar mucha gente

caminando en fila
como hormigas gigantes
sobre senderos de acero

con cámaras digitales
en mano sacándose
muchas fotos entre sí

ignorando las grandes
y pequeñas maravillas
a todo su alrededor

Giant Ants

from our perch
we ants can spot
many people

walking in file
like giant ants
on steel pathways

holding digital cameras
taking lots of photos
of each other

ignoring the great
and tiny wonders
all around them

21

Mejor diversión

recorrer este río
en un gomón
a toda velocidad

acercarse a tumbos
hasta quedar en la base
del trueno de la cascada

para acabar completamente
cacheteados y empapados
por el agua fría del río

supera de veras en mucho
cualquier atracción
de un parque de diversión

Better Fun

cruising this river
on a rubber boat
at full speed

bumping our way
to the base of
the thundering falls

to end up completely
slapped and drenched
by the cool river water

beats by far
any amusement park
attraction

Bendición del Iguazú

acariciándonos
con sus refrescantes
brumas sacras

las cataratas
del Iguazú nos dan
su bendición:

> *vayan en paz*
> *el mundo entero*
> *los espera*

Iguazú Blessing

caressing us
with their refreshing
sacred mist

the Iguazú
waterfalls give us
their blessing:

> *go in peace*
> *the whole world*
> *awaits you*

Mono observador

desde lo más
alto de un árbol
tropical curupay

piensa un mono
capuchino marrón
muy observador:

*¡qué extraños
esos monos
todos vestidos*

*que pasan
trepados arriba
de un gomón!*

Observant Monkey

from the top
of a tropical
curupay tree

a very observant
brown capuchin
monkey thinks:

*how weird are
these monkeys
that all dress up*

*and ride past
on top of
rubber boats!*

Sin fronteras

para todos nosotros
animales silvestres
y plantas de la jungla

no hay límites
sólo una Tierra
sin fronteras

Without Borders

for all of us
wild animals and
plants of the rainforest

there are no limits
only one Earth
without borders

Los bosques

somos el alma
y el corazón
de la Tierra

Forests

we are the soul
and the heart
of the Earth

25

Tierra colorada

Tierra, tienes
tanto hierro
en tu suelo

que tu color
es un colorado
oxidado

como el ají
y el pimiento
secos y molidos

como la canela
y el chocolate
en polvo

Red Earth

Earth, you have
so much iron
in your soil

that your color
is a rusty
red

like ground
dried chiles
and peppers

like cinnamon
and chocolate
powder

River Turtle**

the Southern Hemisphere
travels everywhere
on my hard shell

Tortuga de río*

el Hemisferio Sur
viaja a dondequiera
sobre mi caparazón

* Muchos pueblos indígenas compartían el mito que una gran tortuga cargaba a la Madre Tierra sobre su caparazón a través de las aguas cósmicas del universo.

** Many indigenous peoples of the Americas share the myth that a giant turtle carried Mother Earth on its shell as she swam through the cosmic waters of the universe.

Serenata nocturna

el croc-croc
sin cesar de
nosotros los sapos

llamando
románticamente
a las hembras

es la serenata
nocturna
de la selva

Nightly Serenade

the nonstop
croaking of us
male toads

romantically
calling
the females

is the nightly
serenade
of the jungle

Agua quieta

el agua
antes de caer
en catarata

es tan quieta
como espejo
de cara al cielo

Quiet Water

water before
it plunges down
a waterfall

is as still
as a mirror
facing the sky

Mismo destino verde

escuchemos
la verde voz
de la selva

el coro multicolor
de tantas flores
árboles y aves

aprendamos
los distintos
alfabetos vivientes

de tantas especies
tantos insectos
y mariposas

seamos parte
del clamor y canto
de esta tierra:

*todos ustedes
nos pertenecen como
nosotros a ustedes*

*protéjannos a todos
por el destino de la Tierra
por su propio bien*

sí, hagamos del mundo
una *Ybirá Retá* real—
una Tierra de Árboles

Same Green Fate

let's listen to
the green voice
of the rainforest

the colorful chorus
of so many flowers
trees and birds

let's learn
the distinct
living alphabets

of so many species
so many insects
and butterflies

let's be part
of the clamor and
song of this land:

*you all belong
to us as we all
belong to you*

*protect all of us
for the Earth's fate
for your own sake*

let's make the world
a true *Ybirá Retá—*
a Land of the Trees

For more information about the Iguazú National Park and the tri-national conservation project of the Paranaense rainforest, please contact:

Administración de Parques Nacionales
Av. Tres Fronteras 183 - C.C. 54 – (3370)
Puerto Iguazú, Provincia de Misiones, Argentina
Tel: (54-3757) 421-984/422-906
 E-mail: delegación@parquesnea.com.ar
  www.parquesnacionales.gov.ar

Fundación Vida Silvestre Argentina
Programa Selva Paranaense
Av. Córdoba (N3370COQ)
Puerto Iguazú, Provincia de Misiones, Argentina
Tel: (54-3757) 422-0379
E-mail: vidasilvestre@arnet.com.ar
www.vidasilvestre.org.ar

Photos by Javier Pinzón

Francisco X. Alarcón is a widely acclaimed Chicano poet and educator. His poetry for children has received the Jane Addams Award for Children's Literature and the Pura Belpré Honor Award, among many others. Francisco has also been a finalist for state poet laureate of California. He directs the Spanish for Native Speakers Program at the University of California, Davis.

To Cecilia Colombi, Amparo Argerich, Samiah Hassan, and Margarita Mielnichuk, Argentines who have taught me to love the natural wonders of Argentina and its people. / Para Cecilia Colombi, Amparo Argerich, Samiah Hassan y Margarita Mielnichuk, argentinas que me han enseñado a amar las maravillas naturales de Argentina y a su gente. —FXA

Maya Christina Gonzalez is a fine artist whose work has been featured on the cover of *Contemporary Chicano/a Art*. She has illustrated nearly 20 books for children, many of which have won awards. Her classroom workshops encourage students and teachers to always be fearless in creating art. She lives, paints, and plays in San Francisco, California.

Photo by Marilyn Smith

To Marilyn who plays with me bigger and deeper than anyone has ever played with me; to Zai who teaches me to grow into myself strong and bold; to Raffaele who shows me how beautiful a man can be; and to Kelly who walks like an artist and sings like the sky. To these generous teachers who are my family, I love you; please teach me some more. —MCG

A note about the artwork: I love being in nature. For this book, I wanted to create artwork that in every way brought special attention to my animal friends, who are the focus of these poems. I decided to honor the animals by painting them in a very detailed way, and to use cut paper for the rainforest background and for the people, to show that we are all made up of the same materials... But in one spread I painted the people, because we are animals too. Cutting the water was the most fun of all. —*Maya Christina Gonzalez*

Book design by Carl Angel
Book production by The Kids at Our House
Special thanks to Laura Chastain, Teresa Mlawer, Rosalyn Sheff, and Patricia Villaseñor.

Manufactured in China by First Choice Printing Co. Ltd., May 2015
10 9 8 7 6 5 4 3 2
First Edition

Library of Congress Cataloging-in-Publication Data
Alarcón, Francisco X., 1954-
  Animal poems of the Iguazú: poems / Francisco X. Alarcón; illustrations, Maya Christina Gonzalez = Animalario del Iguazú: poemas / Francisco X. Alarcón; ilustraciones, Maya Christina Gonzalez.
     p. cm.
  ISBN 978-0-89239-299-5 (paperback)
1. Iguaçu Falls (Argentina and Brazil)—Juvenile poetry.
2. Rain forests—Juvenile poetry. 3. Nature—Juvenile poetry. 4. Children's poetry, American. 5. Children's poetry, Hispanic American (Spanish) 6. Children's poetry, American—Translations into Spanish. 7. Children's poetry, Hispanic American (Spanish)—Translations into English. I. Gonzalez, Maya Christina, ill. II. Title. III. Title: Animalario del Iguazú.
  PS3551.L22A85 2008
  811'.54—dc22   2007050011

MIX
Paper from
responsible source
FSC® C02069